KALEIDOSCOPE

THE TRANSCONTINENTAL RAILROAD

by
Edward F. Dolan

BENCHMARK **B**OOKS

MARSHALL CAVENDISH
NEW YORK

Benchmark Books
Marshall Cavendish
99 White Plains Road
Tarrytown, NY 10591

Library of Congress Cataloging-in-Publication Data

Dolan, Edward F., 1924—
The transcontinental railroad / by Edward F. Dolan.
   p.cm. – (Kaleidoscope)
Summary: An exploration of the transcontinental railroad, which became the first rail link between the Atlantic and Pacific
Oceans upon its completion in 1869.
Includes bibliographical references and index.
   ISBN 0-7614-1455-X
1. Railroads—United States—History—Juvenile literature. 2. Pacific railroads—Juvenile literature. [1. Railroads—History. 2.
Pacific railroads.] I. Title. II. Kaleidoscope (Tarrytown, N.Y.)

TF25.P23 D65 2002
385'.0979—dc21
                                    2002000067

Photo Research by Anne Burns Images

Cover Photo by Scala/Art Resource, NY/ Museum of City of New York

The photographs in this book are used by permission and through the courtesy of: *Art Resource, NY*: title page Scala/Museum of
City of New York; *North Wind Pictures*: p. 5, 9, 17, 21, 22, 25, 42; *The Granger Collection, NY*: p. 6, 15, 29, 30, 33, 34, 37; *Nebraska
Historical Society*: p. 10; *Superstock*: p. 13; *Corbis*: p. 14 Medford Historical Society Collection, 41 Bettman; *Denver Public Library*:
p. 18; *Hulton Archive*: p. 26, 38 Frederick Lewis.

Printed in Italy
6 5 4 3 2 1

CONTENTS

RAILS ACROSS THE COUNTRY

On July 1, 1862, Congress took one of the most important steps in the history of the United States. The members passed the Pacific Railroad Act.

The act called for America to build a railroad that would form a link between the Atlantic and Pacific Oceans. Its rails would stretch east from a point in northern California to Omaha, Nebraska.

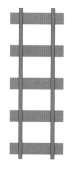

The transcontinental railroad established by the Central Pacific and Union Pacific companies dominates the center of this map. The routes of the Great Northern and Southern Pacific railroads are also shown. The Great Northern spanned America's northern regions, while the Southern Pacific ran through the southwestern states and into the South.

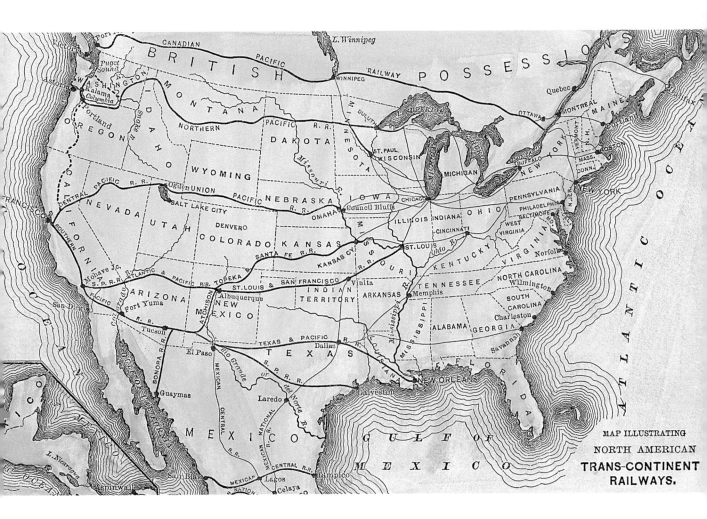

MAP ILLUSTRATING
NORTH AMERICAN
**TRANS-CONTINENT
RAILWAYS.**

As a result, the Pacific Coast would be connected to tracks being built in the eastern half of the country. An iron roadway that stretched clear across the continent would be born—a transcontinental railroad.

Congress named two companies—the Central Pacific and the Union Pacific—to construct the railroad. They planned to lay down tracks that would meet from opposite directions. The Central Pacific tracks would run east from the city of Sacramento, near San Francisco. The Union Pacific tracks would run west from Omaha.

The dream of linking the eastern and western United States with a transcontinental railroad is envisioned in this pen-and-ink cartoon of the late 1860s.

THE CENTRAL PACIFIC RAILROAD

Heading the Central Pacific Railroad were four men who had come to Sacramento during the gold rush of 1849. Mark Hopkins, Collis Huntington, Charles Crocker, and Leland Stanford had made fortunes by starting businesses that sold supplies to the miners.

The four men knew that a transcontinental railroad was vital to the growth of the West. People were constantly arriving in search of gold in California or silver in Nevada. Along with them came an army of settlers who wanted to farm the rich western soil. The arrivals all needed the goods important for everyday life—everything from food and clothing to farming and mining equipment.

Portraits of some of the men behind the construction of the nation's major railroads. They were popularly known as the "railroad barons." Missing is Mark Hopkins of the Central Pacific Railroad.

Oliver Ames.

C. P. Huntington.

Charles Crocker.

Oakes Ames.

Leland Stanford.

Sidney Dillon.

D. H. Moffat.

9

These supplies had to be brought in by ship or wagon train and were slow in reaching their destinations. The four men quickly realized that a railroad was needed to speed their delivery. And they knew that they could make fortunes. They began urging the U.S. government to approve the building of the railroad and to provide money for its construction.

When Congress finally took action after a long debate, it placed the Central Pacific Railroad in their hands. The Union Pacific would be headed by people who purchased stock in the company.

The groundbreaking ceremony at Omaha, Nebraska, that marked the start of the westbound Union Pacific tracks.

Work on the Central Pacific tracks began in Sacramento on January 1863, with Charles Crocker acting as supervisor. The job moved east with agonizing slowness. In two long years, the crews managed to lay tracks only from Sacramento to the foot of the Sierra Nevada mountain range—a distance of less than 50 miles (80.5 kilometers).

The Central Pacific tracks begin to work their way through the foothills of the Sierra Nevada, in northern California. This photograph was taken at a mining camp known as Secret Town, a few miles from Sacramento.

There were reasons for the slow pace. Not only did all the supplies have to be sent west by ship or wagon train, but the country was also caught in the Civil War. The metal and other materials needed for the railroad—everything from sections of track to spikes—had to be used to produce weapons and ammunition for the war.

During the Civil War, the Central Pacific rails were often attacked by both Union and Rebel soldiers. They were uprooted, softened in fires, then wrapped around trees to make them useless to the enemy. Work on the Union Pacific tracks did not begin until the war ended.

Matters improved when the fighting ended in 1865. But soon the workers were faced with an awesome obstacle. Looming high were the Sierra Nevada Mountains. The men spent months struggling in the high thin air. They had to make their way over giant rock walls. In winter, they worked in blinding snowstorms.

The job proved to be backbreaking. Hundreds of men quit as the tracks inched ever higher into the mountains. Recruits became so hard to find that Crocker turned to the workers that he had always shunned—he hired fifty Chinese men on a trial basis.

Winter snows plagued both eastbound and westbound workers. The Central Pacific crews struggled through blizzards in the Sierra Nevada. Pictured here are Union Pacific crews digging a supply train out of a giant snowdrift near Ogden, Utah.

Crocker had previously hired the Chinese to perform the simplest of menial jobs. They had been made to run errands, clean equipment, and help in the kitchens and dining halls. But they worked so hard that he now decided to let them try laying down a section of track.

Crocker was delighted when the Chinese passed his test and proved that they were equal to the job ahead. Further more, he knew that he would not have to pay them as much as his white workers. Finally, he found them unafraid of the dangers that lay ahead—dangers that would take many lives in the coming days. Some men

Chinese immigrants proved to be among the Central Pacific's finest workers.

would be buried alive beneath landslides; some would die in the collapse of tunnels; and some would freeze to death in the winter snows. A newspaper would one day report that the remains of 1,200 Chinese laborers had been sent home during the years of the railroad's construction—about ten tons of bones.

Crocker hired as many Chinese workers as he could find. Soon, the original group of fifty grew to more than two thousand. A short time later, by the summer of 1865, the Central Pacific tracks were snaking high into the Sierras. There, the Chinese met their greatest challenge. It was a challenge that turned into their greatest accomplishment.

The first Chinese workers were so efficient and hardworking that the Central Pacific line began importing workers from all over China.

THE ADVENTURE OF
THE WICKER BASKETS

As the crews inched ever higher, they came upon a stunning sight—a rock formation that thrust upward 4,000 feet (1,219 meters) from its base. The workers quickly dubbed it Cape Horn, after the real Cape Horn that lay at the foot of South America. The rock formation was a giant obstacle that could have ended the work on the Central Pacific Railroad.

Laborers worked together under very dangerous conditions.

There was only one way to get past Cape Horn. Workers had to cut a roadbed through the high rock wall. The job terrified most of the workers.

But not the Chinese. Crocker shipped in bundles of thin wooden strips, which the Chinese workers wove into a number of baskets. The finished baskets carried two men each and were lowered down the rock wall by rope. There, while dangling several thousand feet in the air, the two-man crews spent weeks drilling holes in the stone and filling them with explosives. When the explosives were detonated, the baskets were yanked, getting the Chinese to safety before great chunks of the wall went flying in all directions. Thirty-seven Chinese laborers lost their lives while doing this dangerous but necessary work.

Construction crews work on the entrance to one of the fifteen tunnels that had to be cut through the Sierra Nevada.

The job of fashioning the roadbed lasted from mid-1865 to the spring of 1866. The challenge was a mighty one, but others soon followed. For one, the crews cut fifteen tunnels through the mountains of the Sierra Nevada. For another, they created almost 40 miles (64.4 kilometers) of wooden sheds, or "tunnels," along the mountainsides to keep the track free of snow during the winter.

At last, the workers—white and Chinese—put the heights of the Sierra Nevada behind them and entered Nevada, which had become a state in 1864. Then, as they speared eastward across the desert, they caught sight of dust in the distance—a sign that the Union Pacific work crews were approaching.

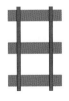

Once they put the peaks of the Sierra Nevada behind them, the Central Pacific crews swiftly laid tracks across Nevada's high desert, advancing several miles a day.

THE UNION PACIFIC RAILROAD

On December 2, 1863, the Union Pacific Railroad held groundbreaking ceremonies at what was then the small town of Omaha, Nebraska. Unfortunately, due to financial problems, not a single section of track was laid for another two years. The company, which was headed by Thomas Durant of New York City, finally got down to work at the close of the Civil War, in early 1865.

Thomas Durant headed the Union Pacific Railroad. He was a physician who, upon his graduation from medical school, chose to enter the stock market rather than practice medicine. Though he became a wealthy and successful businessman, he always delighted in being addressed as "Doctor."

29

In May of 1866, when just 40 miles (64.4 kilometers) of track had been laid, the Union Pacific hired General Grenville Dodge to be the new chief engineer, hoping he would hasten the construction. Dodge, a soldier and engineer, had been granted army leave to take the post. He and his crews were soon considering a special spot in the approaching Rocky Mountains—a path called South Pass, which ran between the towering peaks. It was a gap that westbound covered wagons had used for years. It would now carry the nation's trains.

Chinese and white crews lay tracks through South Pass, a path through the Rocky Mountains.

There were more than ten thousand men laying track as the pass came into view. They were accompanied by railroad trains and horse-drawn wagons that hauled in iron rails, wooden ties, and tons of working equipment daily. Also following the work gangs was a train of more than twenty rail cars. They carried blacksmith and carpenter shops, water tanks, mess halls, and sleeping quarters for the workers.

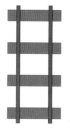

The train and horse-drawn wagons that accompanied the Union Pacific workers supplied the men with everything from rails and tools to dining halls and sleeping quarters. Similar trains and wagons also traveled with the Central Pacific crews.

By October 1866, the tracks extended 247 miles (397 kilometers) west of Omaha. Two years later, the rails were progressing through the Rockies, past Ogden, Utah. By 1869, they were coming down from the heights and running across the Utah desert.

The construction was moving quickly, but it was not free of trouble. The Indians who lived in the surrounding areas became increasingly angry at the passing rails. They saw their buffalo herds being wiped out to feed the crews and to provide visiting tourists with sport. They saw the lands of their ancestors being violated. They began ambushing work crews and ripping up sections of track.

In this French engraving, Sioux Indians attack a Union Pacific work train.

During one incident, a band of Cheyenne found a railroad tie lying next to the track. They lashed it to the rails and then watched as a train came puffing through the night. It derailed and crashed into the desert. On another occasion, a large band of Sioux attacked a work gang and killed all five of its members.

Problems with the Indians lessened through the years and then disappeared when the Cheyenne were overcome by U.S. troops. Treaties with the Indians put an end to other hostilities.

Indians sabotaged the railroad crews for many months. The attacks caused so much damage, injury, and death that army troops were assigned to guard the work crews. Before the trouble ended, U.S. officials held a number of peace conferences with tribal representatives, such as the one photographed here, at Fort Laramie, Wyoming, in 1868.

37

THE WORK IS COMPLETED

The morning of May 10, 1869, was cloudy and cold at Promontory Point, Utah. The point stood on the northern shore of the Great Salt Lake. It was to go down in American history as the place where the nation's transcontinental railroad was finally completed. There, 1,086 miles (1,748 kilometers) of track laid down by Union Pacific crews and 689 miles (1,109 kilometers) by Central Pacific workers were about to be joined.

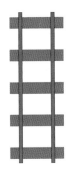

Workers joined with railroad officials to commemorate the completion of the transcontinental railroad. For the ceremony, locomotives from the two railroads were brought to within a few feet of each other and christened with champagne. Facing each other on the opposite page are the Central Pacific's Jupiter *and the Union Pacific's* No. 119. *The* Jupiter *burned coal, while* No. 119 *was a wood-burner.*

A crowd of workmen and spectators cheered as the engines of the two railroads approached each other and braked to a halt. Workers carried a block of laurel wood from the Central Pacific train; it was to be the final tie in the new railroad. Leland Stanford and Thomas Durant, the heads of the Central Pacific and the Union Pacific, watched closely as it was put into place.

Four special spikes—two of California gold, one of Nevada silver, and one a mixture of iron, silver, and gold from Arizona—were brought to Stanford and Durant. The men took turns trying to drive the spikes into the final tie. Both missed!

When both Leland Stanford of the Central Pacific and Thomas Durant of the Union Pacific missed driving the last four spikes that would join the two railroads together, General Jack Casement, the Union Pacific's construction boss, finished the job for them.

Amid laughter from the surrounding crowd, a workman stepped forward. A moment later—at 12:47 P.M.—the spikes were in place. Cheers went echoing across the Great Salt Lake.

The people present did not know it, but the special tie and the four spikes would be removed and replaced with substitutes—to keep them safe from theft. But even if they had known, it would not have silenced their cheers. America's transcontinental railroad was finally a reality.

The Civil War had slowed the expansion westwards of the United States. Now that expansion would be reborn along miles of steel rails.

When finally linked, the tracks ran 1,086 miles (1,748 kilometers) west from the Missouri River and 689 miles (1,109 kilometers) east from Sacramento, California. Americans could now travel clear across the country by rail.

43

1840s–1850s

Congress argues over possible routes for a transcontinental railroad.

1862

Congress chooses a route from Nebraska to northern California during the Civil War. President Abraham Lincoln signs the Pacific Railroad Act on July 1.

1863

Groundbreaking ceremonies to mark the start of work on the Union Pacific Railroad take place at Omaha on December 2.

1864

Groundbreaking ceremonies for the Central Pacific Railroad are held at Sacramento on January 8, followed soon by the laying of the line's first track.

In June, the Central Pacific publishes its first timetable, announcing passenger and freight service over a stretch of thirty-one miles out of Sacramento.

The Union Pacific begins to lay track west from Omaha in July. The late start is due to money problems.

1865

The Civil War ends.

1869

The tracks of the two railroads meet in the desert at Promontory Point on the shores of the Great Salt Lake in Utah on May 10.

FIND OUT MORE

BOOKS

Best, Gerald M. *Iron Horses to Promontory*. San Marino, California: Golden West, 1969.

Blumberg, Rhoda. *Full Steam Ahead: The Race to Build a Transcontinental Railroad*. Washington, D.C.: National Geographic Society, 1996.

Brinkley, Douglas. *American Heritage History of the United States*. New York: Viking, 1998.

Galloway, John. *The First Transcontinental Railroad*. New York: Dorset Press, 1990.

Klein, Maury. *Union Pacific: Birth of a Railroad, 1862–93*. New York: Walker, 1987.

Williams, John Hoyt. *A Great and Shining Road: The Epic Story of the Transcontinental Railroad*. New York: Times Books, 1988.

ORGANIZATIONS & WEB SITES

The Union Pacific Railroad
www.uprr.com/aboutup/history/

The American Experience: The Iron Road
www.pbs.org/wgbh/amex/iron/

The Central Pacific Railroad
http://cprr.org/Museum/index.html

Edward F. Dolan is the author of over one hundred nonfiction books for young people and adults. He has written on medicine, science, law, history, folklore, and current social issues. Mr. Dolan is a native Californian, born in the San Francisco region, and raised in Southern California. In addition to writing books, he has been a newspaper reporter and a magazine editor. He currently lives in the northern part of the state.

INDEX

Page numbers for illustrations are in boldface.